SRA

Open Court Reading

Nat

A Division of The McGraw·Hill Companies

Columbus, Ohio

www.sra4kids.com

SRA/McGraw-Hill

*A Division of The **McGraw·Hill** Companies*

Send all inquiries to:
SRA/McGraw-Hill
8787 Orion Place
Columbus, OH 43240-4027

ISBN 0-07-569421-2
1 2 3 4 5 6 7 8 9 DBH 05 04 03 02 01

Nat naps.

Nan hits a tin pan.
Nat naps and naps.

Pam tips a tin pan.
Nat naps and naps and naps.

An ant sits by Nat.
An ant taps Nat.

Nat sits.

Nat naps and naps.